POINTS OF VIEW

I0794144

Should Social Media Have AGE LIMITS?

By Elizabeth Morgan

KidHaven PUBLISHING

Published in 2024 by
KidHaven Publishing, an Imprint of Greenhaven Publishing, LLC
2544 Clinton St.
Buffalo, NY 14224

Designer: Deanna Paternostro
Editor: Katie Kawa

Photo credits: Cover Chinnapong/Shutterstock.com; p. 5 Zivica Kerkez/Shutterstock.com; pp. 7, 21 (inset, right) Ground Picture/Shutterstock.com; p. 9 Potstock/Shutterstock.com; pp. 11, 19 fizkes/Shutterstock.com; p. 13 SpeedKingz/Shutterstock.com; p. 15 SeventyFour/Shutterstock.com; p. 17 katarinag/Shutterstock.com; p. 21 (notepad) ESB Professional/Shutterstock.com; p. 21 (markers) Kucher Serhii/Shutterstock.com; p. 21 (photo frame) FARBAI/iStock/Thinkstock; p. 21 (inset, left) Prostock-studio/Shutterstock.com; p. 21 (inset, middle) Antonio Guillem/Shutterstock.com.

Library of Congress Cataloging-in-Publication Data

Names: Morgan, Elizabeth, author.
Title: Should social media have age limits? / Elizabeth Morgan.
Description: Buffalo, New York : KidHaven Publishing, [2024] | Series: Points of view | Includes bibliographical references and index.
Identifiers: LCCN 2023004379 | ISBN 9781534545168 (library binding) | ISBN 9781534545151 (paperback) | ISBN 9781534545175 (ebook)
Subjects: LCSH: Social media–Juvenile literature. | Internet–Safety measures–Juvenile literature. | Internet access–Juvenile literature. | Internet and children–Juvenile literature.
Classification: LCC HM742 .M67 2024 | DDC 302.23/1–dc23/eng/20230310
LC record available at https://lccn.loc.gov/2023004379

Printed in the United States of America

Some of the images in this book illustrate individuals who are models. The depictions do not imply actual situations or events.

CPSIA compliance information: Batch #CSKH24: For further information contact Greenhaven Publishing LLC at 1-844-317-7404.

CONTENTS

What's Social Media? 4
An Important Law 6
Safety First! 8
Who Knows Best? 10
Bullies Online 12
Making Friends 14
Harmful for Mental Health 16
Do They Work? 18
Many Different Opinions 20
Glossary 22
For More Information 23
Index 24

What's SOCIAL MEDIA?

Social media is a big part of our world today. It's a collection of websites and apps, or applications, that allow users to connect with each other and create online communities. Many adults use social media, but they're not the only ones. In fact, more young people than ever are using social media.

The continued rise in social media use among kids and teens has made many people think about age limits for these **platforms**. Is it good to have them, or should young people be given the freedom to make their own social media choices?

Know the Facts!

A 2021 study showed that 38 percent of kids between the ages of 8 and 12 have used social media at some point in their lives.

Before you form your own opinion about social media age limits, it's helpful to learn more about this issue so you can back up your feelings with facts.

An Important LAW

Most social media platforms currently have age limits in place. For most platforms, including TikTok, Instagram, Tumblr, and Facebook, young people must be at least 13 years old to create an account, which allows them to post and **interact** on the platform.

This age limit is in place because of a federal, or national, law that was written in 1998. This law is called the Children's Online Privacy Protection Act (COPPA). It led to an important rule that said online companies couldn't collect personal **information** from kids younger than 13 years old without a parent or guardian's permission.

Know the Facts!

YouTube is considered a social media platform because people can create videos and like or **comment** on other users' videos. Although very young kids often watch YouTube videos, you must be at least 13 years old to create an account, which allows you to post and interact on YouTube.

Many people believe parents, especially parents of young kids, should know what their kids are doing online. COPPA was created to help parents make informed, or educated, choices about what websites their kids are allowed to visit.

Safety FIRST!

COPPA was created to help make the internet safer for kids. Safety is still a big concern, or worry, for adults when it comes to their children and social media. One reason why they often support age limits for social media platforms is because they believe these limits help keep kids safe.

Social media age limits can keep kids from talking to adults who might be dangerous, or unsafe. These limits can also **protect** kids' privacy, since the companies that run social media platforms often collect information about users, such as their name and birthdate. This information could later be stolen.

Know the Facts!

Social media platforms are often filled with **advertisements**, or ads, that are shown to users based on information the platform has collected about them. It can be hard to tell the difference between ads and posts that aren't ads, especially for kids.

It's important for everyone to know basic online safety tips. Always tell a trusted adult if a person says something to you online that makes you uncomfortable. Also, don't share personal information, such as your full name or address.

Who Knows BEST?

Most people agree that safety is the most important thing when it comes to kids on the internet. However, some adults disagree that the best way to keep kids safe is with age limits. They believe freedom is important, especially online.

People who don't support social media age limits believe it should be up to parents and guardians to decide if their kids can use social media. They feel it's a personal decision to be made within a family and not something social media companies should decide for everyone.

Know the Facts!

Many devices, websites, and apps allow adults to use parental controls. These are settings that parents or guardians can use to control what their children see online, including what websites they can visit.

Many parents and guardians make their own rules for social media use, including at what age a child can get their first social media account and what platform it can be on.

Bullies ONLINE

Social media can be used to make friends, but it can also be used by bullies. Cyberbullying is a big problem, and people are looking for ways to stop it. One idea is keeping kids off social media, which is where a lot of cyberbullying takes place.

Young people care a lot about what others think of them—wanting to be liked is a basic part of growing up. It's hard for them to handle mean social media comments. They also might be more likely to join in if a group is cyberbullying someone, because they want to fit in.

Know the Facts!

According to a 2019 study, 1 out of every 3 young people in 30 countries around the world has reported being cyberbullied.

Many adults are hurt by mean comments on social media, and sometimes adults say hurtful things to others online because they can do so without anyone knowing who they really are. Some people believe kids shouldn't be allowed on social media because they're less **mature** than adults and would have an even harder time with these things.

Making FRIENDS

Social media isn't all good or all bad. For example, while cyberbullying is a problem on social media, these platforms can also help kids who are dealing with bullies or who feel lonely. Social media platforms allow people to connect with others who have the same interests, even if they live far apart.

This is one reason why some people believe social media shouldn't have age limits. It can be a helpful tool for kids who are having a hard time making friends. Their online community can make them feel supported, safe, and happy.

Know the Facts!

A 2022 study showed that 67 percent of U.S. teens said social media helps them feel like they have people supporting them during hard times.

Social media gives kids an outlet for their creativity. They can create and share things like videos, drawings, and pieces of writing with others who will support them.

Harmful for MENTAL HEALTH

In some cases, social media can help kids' **mental** health by making them feel less alone. However, many people argue that it's much more likely for social media to have a harmful effect on kids' mental health.

People often compare themselves to what they see on social media, which can lead to feelings of **anxiety** and **depression**. Posts on social media are often carefully created to show only the best things about someone's life. However, it's hard for kids to understand this, which can lead them to feel bad about themselves.

Know the Facts!

Social media is connected to body image, or how we see our bodies, especially for girls. Pictures on social media are often edited, or changed, but young girls might think their body could and should look like the bodies in edited pictures. This can lead them to feel bad about how they look.

Cases of anxiety and depression are on the rise in young people between the ages of 3 and 17. Some people believe social media use is a big part of this problem. They've argued that no one under 16—or even 18—years old should be allowed to use certain social media sites to protect the mental health of young people.

Do They WORK?

Social media causes problems for a lot of kids even with the current age limits in place. This has led many people to argue that age limits don't really work to protect kids from the dangers of social media. There are age limits now, but many kids younger than 13 are still active on social media.

It's hard to **enforce** social media age limits. Kids can lie when creating an account and say they're older than they really are. People sometimes argue that the rules in place today are so easily broken that it's like they don't exist at all.

Know the Facts!

As of 2019, one in five U.S. kids had their own smartphone by the time they were eight years old.

When kids have their own devices, such as smartphones or tablets, that can have social media apps, it makes it easier to get past the age limits for these apps.

Many Different OPINIONS

People have many different opinions about social media age limits. Some people think they're fine as they are right now and shouldn't change. Others think the age limit should be higher—as high as 18 years old. Still others argue that social media age limits are too easy for kids to get around, so the issue should be left up to parents to decide.

It's important for you to form your own opinions about issues that **affect** you, such as if and when you can use social media. So, what do you think? Should social media have age limits?

Know the Facts!

Social media played an important part in keeping people connected during the **COVID-19 pandemic**. A 2021 study showed an increase in the number of kids between the ages of 8 and 12 using social media after the pandemic began in 2020.

Should social media have age limits?

YES

- Age limits on social media help keep kids from talking with adults who might be dangerous.
- Age limits protect kids' personal information, which can be collected on social media platforms.
- Age limits for social media can help stop cyberbullying.
- Social media can be harmful for kids' mental health.

NO

- Parents should have the freedom to decide if their child is old enough to use social media.
- Parental controls can be used instead of age limits.
- Kids should be allowed on social media because it can give them a safe support system if they feel bullied or lonely.
- Age limits don't really work online.

Making a chart such as this one can help you more clearly understand different points of view.

GLOSSARY

advertisement: A public notice that is created to make people want to buy a good or service.

affect: To produce an effect on something.

anxiety: A mental condition marked by strong feelings of fear or nervousness about what might happen.

comment: To make a statement of opinion about something. Also, a statement of opinion about something.

COVID-19 pandemic: An event that began in China in 2019 in which a disease that causes breathing problems, a fever, and other health issues spread rapidly around the world and made millions of people sick in a short period of time.

depression: A mental health condition in which a person feels very sad, hopeless, and unimportant and is often unable to do basic tasks because of this.

enforce: To make sure people do what is required by a rule or law.

information: Knowledge or facts about something.

interact: To come together and have an effect on each other.

mature: Having the qualities of an adult.

mental: Relating to the mind.

platform: An application or website that serves as a base from which a service is provided.

protect: To keep safe.

For More INFORMATION

WEBSITES

How to Deal with "Haters"
www.stopbullying.gov/cyberbullying/how-to-deal-with-haters
This part of the U.S. government's antibullying website offers advice on what to do if you are dealing with a cyberbully or a mean commenter online.

KidsHealth: Online Safety
kidshealth.org/en/kids/online-id.html
Visit this website to learn social media safety tips.

BOOKS

Anthony, William. *Learn the Language of Social Media.* New York, NY: Enslow Publishing, 2022.

Dell, Pamela. *Understanding Social Media.* North Mankato, MN: Capstone Press, 2019.

Gregory, Josh. *Posting on Social Media.* New York, NY: Children's Press, 2019.

Publisher's note to educators and parents: Our editors have carefully reviewed these websites to ensure that they are suitable for students. Many websites change frequently, however, and we cannot guarantee that a site's future contents will continue to meet our high standards of quality and educational value. Be advised that students should be closely supervised whenever they access the Internet.

INDEX

A
ads, 8
anxiety, 16, 17
apps, 4, 10, 19

B
body image, 16

C
Children's Online Privacy Protection Act (COPPA), 6, 7, 8
comments, 6, 12, 13
COVID-19 pandemic, 20
cyberbullying, 12, 14, 21

D
depression, 16, 17

F
Facebook, 6

I
Instagram, 6

M
mental health, 16, 17, 21

P
parental controls, 10, 21
privacy, 8

S
smartphones, 18, 19

T
TikTok, 6
Tumblr, 6

Y
YouTube, 6